Speaking Out About My Disability

AN AUTOBIOGRAPHY
LARRY E. APPELMANN

National Library of Canada Cataloguing in Publication

Appelmann, Larry E. (Larry Edward)
 Living with spina bifida : speaking out about my
disability / Larry E. Appelmann.
ISBN 1-55395-069-0
 I. Title.
RJ496.S74A66 2002   362.1'989283   C2002-904360-3

TRAFFORD

This book was published *on-demand* in cooperation with Trafford Publishing.
On-demand publishing is a unique process and service of making a book available for retail sale to the public taking advantage of on-demand manufacturing and Internet marketing.
On-demand publishing includes promotions, retail sales, manufacturing, order fulfilment, accounting and collecting royalties on behalf of the author.

2404 Government St., Victoria, B.C. V8T 4L7, CANADA

Phone	250-383-6864	Toll-free	1-888-232-4444 (Canada & US)
Fax	250-383-6804	E-mail	sales@trafford.com
Web site	www.trafford.com	TRAFFORD PUBLISHING IS A DIVISION OF TRAFFORD HOLDINGS LTD.	
Trafford Catalogue #02-0783	www.trafford.com/robots/02-0783.html		

10   9   8   7   6   5   4   3

To my family and friends who helped me to be the best I am today; without them, who knows where I would be and what I would be. I would especially like to thank all of the teachers who taught me to be the kind of person that I am today.

Larry E. Appelmann

Table of Content

PROLOGUE

Sometimes the words angry, frustrated, scared, happy, and sad, might describe how I feel being handicapped and not having the chance to do things that I would like to be able to do because of my disability. Sometimes words just cannot describe how I really feel.

I don't blame anybody for the cause of my disability, because when I was born, a disability like mine couldn't be prevented. Even if it could have been, I still would not blame anybody. I wish that I could change the way things are, but I can't. To be honest with you I would give anything if I could walk.

Many people don't know about or even stop to realize the type of dedication and help that people like me have to have because of my physical disability.

Throughout this book, I will be telling you about all of the surgeries that I have had throughout my life and why they were necessary. I will also tell you about how I got to where I am today and the things that I enjoy doing every chance that I get. One of the things you will discover about me is that it has never bothered me when people have asked me about my disability. The only time that I will talk about my disability is when people ask me about it, which makes me think they are interested in knowing more about my disability. The hardest part about my disability is how to explain it so that people will understand. I'm just glad that people like me for who I am and not what I am. I used to be uncomfortable talking about my disability, but now discussing it doesn't bother me.

I hope you will sit back, relax, and enjoy reading this book and I hope you will be able to understand some, or perhaps all, of the things in my autobiography.

I hardly remember some of the things that have happened to me in the past, but there is one thing that I know for sure. I have been through a lot, and I'm still here. As far as I am concerned, that is the only thing that really counts.

1

MY BIRTH

It all began on August 16, 1980, when I was born at Mercy Hospital in Mariemont, Ohio. Shortly after I was born, the doctors discovered a hole in my back where the spine is located. The doctors told my mother and father that the hole in my back was about the size of a quarter.

They explained to my parents that this opening in my back was known as spina bifida, and that surgery was required as soon as possible to close it up so that I would not develop spinal meningitis.

Within a matter of hours, I was taken to Children's Hospital in Cincinnati, Ohio to have the surgery. The surgery was done by pulling the skin around the hole, and then sewing it shut.

The surgery was a complete success, but because of the spina bifida, the doctors told my parents that I would only have about a 50-percent chance of walking. They also said that I might end up being mentally retarded. In the beginning, my mother and father did not know what spina bifida was, but as time went on, they learned what it was and how to deal with it.

Several weeks after the surgery, I was still in the hospital when they had to do another surgery to place a shunt into my head to regulate the flow of spinal fluid. The shunt is connected by putting it inside the skin, through the skull and into the abdominal wall. The spinal fluid is then absorbed into the body tissue.

After the doctors put in the shunt, they had to keep a close eye on it so that they would know how well it was working. They monitored the shunt's performance by measuring the size of my head.

A shunt is a medical device that is made of synthetic material. The shunt has a relief valve that allows the right amount of spinal fluid to flow from the brain.

Having too much fluid on the brain or not enough eventually leads to a serious medical problem if it is not treated immediately. This started to happen to me when I was about 14 or 15 years old, but I will tell you more about that later.

Shortly after the shunt had been put in, my parents were told by the doctors to be aware of symptoms such as convulsions, nausea, headaches and changes in behavior. Some other signs of a shunt malfunction could include refusal to eat, projectile vomiting, uncharacteristic irritability or unusual sensitivity to noises, dizziness, fever, confusion, loss of balance, visual problems, pain in the neck area, tremors of the hand(s) or the eyelid(s), and periods of total body rigidity.

These first surgeries are just two of the many that I have had over the years to help me live a better and easier life, and to help me avoid serious medical problems later on.

Because of these two surgeries, I had to stay in the hospital for approximately one month. Afterwards, my mother and father were finally able to take me home to start taking care of me the best way that they knew how.

My parents had a family physician who said that they should contact him anytime they needed help or in case of an emergency. He decided that it would be better to send me to another physician, because he didn't know enough about spina bifida to be certain what to do when I needed to have medical attention, and he was concerned about not being able to do the best for me.

One of the things my doctors told my parents to do was to take special care of my kidneys and bladder. Without this kind of special care, I would have to deal with serious medical problems, such as bladder infections.

2

SPINA BIFIDA: WHAT IS IT?

The medical term for spina bifida is Myelomeningocele, which is a word that I sometimes cannot even pronounce. Spina bifida is a Latin word meaning, "split spine". It is also the name that has been given to a group of birth defects that can possibly interfere with the development of the central nervous system, the brain, the spinal cord, and the nerve tissue.

Spina bifida is a birth defect, which usually happens for an unknown reason. The causes of spina bifida are not yet completely understood. Since 1996, studies have shown that women, who are planning on getting pregnant or women who are already pregnant, should begin to take approximately 0.4 milligrams of vitamin B folic acid each day, which will help to prevent a birth defect such as spina bifida. When I was born, my mother and father were not aware of this information because the study was not published until 1996. Every year, about 1,500 babies, or one in every 2,000, are born with this condition, and as of now, there is no known cure for spina bifida. Children born with spina bifida are also born with the spinal column only partially closed, so it has to be closed surgically.

There are three types of spina bifida: Occulta,

Meningocele, and Myelomeningocele. The extensis of the paralysis depends upon the size of the hole.

The type of spina bifida that I was born with is Myelomeningocele. This type of spina bifida is the most severe and disabling of the three. In this condition, both the spinal cord and the meninges are pushed out through an opening in the vertebral column. Then a thin, fluid filled sac or cyst covers the area where the spinal cord is pushed out, which causes a certain degree of paralysis in the legs, and bladder and bowel dysfunction. For instance, if I broke my leg I would not know it because I wouldn't be able to feel the pain.

Because of my paralysis, I don't have any feeling from the waist down. Technically, my paralysis begins at the fifth lumbar vertebra, so to get around, I have to use a wheelchair. My neurosurgeon thought that I would end up being mentally retarded because of my condition, but he was wrong.

I didn't start learning how to use a wheelchair until I was about two years old. Until then, I just crawled around on the floor. My parents tried to get me to learn how to use leg braces and a walker instead of a wheelchair, but I just didn't have the strength and my sense of balance wasn't what it was supposed to be either.

When I was about three years old, I did start to learn how to use leg braces and a walker. Over the years, I continued to try using the leg braces and walker from time to time but I had to wear a plastic upper body brace to stabilize myself. However, I no longer use leg braces.

I was also born with a spinal curvature called scoliosis. This occurs as muscle paralysis frequently intensifies the condition because some of the muscles in the body tighten if they are not being used. If the muscles that are attached to the spinal column tighten, they tend to pull the vertebrae in several different directions, where normally, vertebrae of the same size and shape are stacked one on top of the other.

In most cases, people born with spina bifida can also have one or more vertebrae that can be malformed, wedge shaped or fused together, or a combination of both. This upsets the straight line of the spinal column, causing the spinal curvature.

There are three types of spinal curvature: "Scoliosis," which is what I have, "Kyphosis" and "Lordosis." Kyphosis occurs when there are no muscles to pull the spinal column in the thoracic region so it is bent or curved outward. This tends to pull the chest toward the legs and push the stomach into the lungs. People who have this type of spinal curvature often have difficulty breathing. Kyphosis develops in eight to 15 percent of children born with spina bifida

Scoliosis is the most common spinal curvature in people born with spina bifida, and in the general population. An S-shaped curvature and sideways bending of the spine is what known as scoliosis. The spinal curvature isn't really noticeable until about two or three years of age. It is also possible for scoliosis to develop because of malformed vertebrae, or because of a shunt malfunction.

If cerebral spinal fluid (CSF), which protects the brain from the skull, is allowed to accumulate inside of the brain and the spinal cord, a condition known as "Hydromyelia" occurs where the fluid that gets built up inside the spinal column starts to weaken some of the muscles and nerves.

If the spinal column shifts forward in the lumbar region, "Lordosis" occurs. To compensate for this curvature, the body will automatically push the stomach into an outward position, which is also, what happened to me.

For people like me born with a spinal curvature, there are two options of treatment. The first option is to make a molded plastic jacket or brace, which helps to provide support for the spinal column and helps decrease the amount of the curvature and the stress in the spine.

The second option is surgery, which fuses the vertebrae together by using steel rods, cables or sometimes plates and then screwing them to the spinal column to help hold them in place. This type of procedure can take eight hours or more.

When I was seven years old, the doctors had to put two steel rods in my back, each about three sixteenths of an inch in diameter. They also took pieces of bone from my legs and put them in my back in order to form the correct structure of my back.

Before they could do my back surgery, they first had to break my legs to loosen up the tendons. This was done with a laser beam. After the back surgery, I was placed into a body cast for about six months. When the body cast was taken off, I had to wear a plastic upper body brace for approximately one year. To make things even more interesting, I had the chicken pox while I was in the body cast.

This spinal fusion makes a segment of the spinal column rigid and prevents further curvature. Unfortunately, spinal curvature can also decrease growth. My doctors didn't think that I would grow much as a result of this operation, but I grew taller than they thought I would.

Initially, the spinal surgery had to be postponed for a while because I repeatedly ran a fever that would go away and then come back again every time my parents took me to the hospital to have the surgery. This happened twice before my doctors made the decision to postpone the surgery for six months to see if the fever would go away.

In the mean time, a plastic brace was made for me to wear to prevent further curvature problems. It was about a year before the surgery actually took place.

Five years later, when I was 12 years old and in the fifth grade, the rods that were placed in my back had broken. That meant that the doctors had to perform another back surgery as soon as possible.

During my second back surgery, they removed broken pieces of steel rods from my back, and instead of inserting new rods; they put in a steel plate and took a piece of shinbone from my legs for bone graphting.

Bone graphting involves placing pieces of bone to the affected area for reinforcement. Because the surgery took place during my fifth grade year in school, and I was placed into another body cast, I home schooled after the surgery.

After the first back surgery, they used sutures, which are stitches that dissolve instead of staples because they immediately put me into a body cast. The body cast I had after the second surgery went all the way up to my arms. This was when I contracted the chicken pox. The body cast from my first back surgery went all the way up to my neck, but they didn't have to put staples in my back for the second surgery. I have heard my parents say many times that if you were to look at an x-ray of my back, you might compare it to a hardware store because of all the metal rods and screws and whatever else might be in there.

People born with spina bifida usually have allergies to things such as latex and other rubber products. So far, I don't seem to have any allergies, which the doctors say is very rare.

3

SHUNTS: WHAT ARE THEY?

In case you don't know what a shunt is, read on! A shunt is a tube that drains the CSF from the ventricles in the head into another part of the body where the fluid is then absorbed. The abdominal cavity, which is the space around the stomach and intestines, is most often used. The shunt's small, soft tubing is placed or tunneled under the skin, and the end of the tubing is then placed in the abdominal space.

A relief valve, which is attached to the shunt tubing, controls the flow and direction of the cerebral spinal fluid in order to keep a normal amount of CSF inside the ventricles. This helps to prevent Hydrocephalus or too much fluid on the brain, which occurs in about 50 to 70 percent of people born with Myelomeningocele.

Hydrocephalus can also occur in children who are not born with spina bifida when the cerebral spinal fluid, which is used for cushioning and protecting the brain and spinal cord, is unable to drain successfully because of a spinal defect.

Sometimes when shunts do not function properly all or part of the shunt must be replaced. The neurosurgeon then must identify the problem within the shunt system and decide if replacing the shunt is necessary.

If the shunt has malfunctioned and is to be replaced, the neurosurgeon will then have to replace either the PROXIMAL TUBING, which is the tubing in the head, or the DISTAL TUBING, which is the tubing to the abdominal space, and/or the valve, which is located around the neck area. This happened to me when my shunt somehow became disconnected when I was about 13 or 14 years old.

A shunt malfunction could be caused by the build-up of body tissue or proteins, and certain chemicals may also cause the cerebral spinal fluid to be blocked away from the brain, which might clog the shunt tubing. Over a long period of time the shunt tubing may wear itself out or pull itself apart, requiring it to be replaced, which is what happened to me.

When I was 16 years old, instead of replacing the shunt, my neurosurgeon used an alternative procedure called an Endoscopic Third Ventriculostomy. Using a laser, known as the KTP/532 Wavelength, and a long skinny camera, called an endoscope, he created an incision at the top of my head. The Endoscope was then passed to guide the laser as it formed a small drainage canal at the base of my neck. This type of surgery is expected to be a more reliable and permanent fix and is becoming a more common procedure than shunt replacement.

The surgery was necessary because I was starting to experience symptoms such as constant headaches, dizziness, eye twitching, and vomiting, as well as a change in my behavior and school grades.

The doctor did not immediately recommend surgery. Instead, he decided to keep me in the hospital for a few days to run some tests to discover if the shunt was still working or not. I stayed in the hospital for at least three days, having tests such as MRIs, ultrasounds, x-rays, and CTs to help if I needed to have the surgery.

They also performed a spinal fluid test, which is done by sticking a needle, inside near the shunt valve to drain some spinal fluid. This test was the most painful. It seemed like that it was taking forever for it to end. Actually, the test took only about twenty minutes. Having this spinal fluid test done also made me get very upset because I do not like needles at all.

This test and the ultrasound test that they performed apparently were inconclusive. The doctors and nurses were unable to see the shunt well enough to establish how much spinal fluid was passing through because over a long period of time, bones that grew over the shunt were covering it up the shunt, making it difficult to see anything going on inside.

Every test that was done at the hospital showed very little signs of spinal fluid flowing. The negative test results made me angry because I felt like that I went through all of those tests for no reason. The test results were sufficient for my doctor to make the decision that the surgery would have to be done as soon as possible because of my symptoms and because the shunt had stopped functioning.

The Endoscopic surgery was done on February 7, 1997 around 7:30 a.m, which meant that I needed to be at the hospital around 6:30 a.m.

This surgery occurred during my first year in high school. It was only a minor procedure but I did spend a couple of days in the hospital. I could have gone back to school after the surgery but I didn't go back for approximately a week because of a terrible headache.

Normally, shunts are only expected to last for only about two or three years until things start to go wrong. I was lucky because mine did not quit working until I was about 14 years old and my doctors do not know for sure exactly when my shunt stopped working.

Since the surgery, everything has improved. My grades are higher, I haven't had the types of headaches that were associated with a shunt malfunction, I haven't gotten as sick as I used to, I have my appetite back, I can think better, and I can also concentrate easier. Thanks to my doctor, I should not have to worry about these problems any longer.

4

THE EARLY YEARS

Most children don't start school until they are about six or seven years old, but in 1982, when I was only about two years old, until 1987, when I was about seven years old, my parents sent me to morning preschool for two days a week. For a few years, instead of letting me ride the school bus, my mother would drive me to and from school and would stay at school with me.

The school is now named Thomas Wildey, but used to be called Clermont County Special Education Training Center. This school is a special individual educational training school for children that are mentally and/or physically handicapped.

My doctors recommended this school to my parents because they thought that I would need to have certain specialized treatment, such as physical therapy, and this school was the only one around that provided this for children at such a young age.

When I started going to this school, one of the first things that my teachers began to do was teach me sign language. The teachers never told my parents that I would never be able to talk; they wanted to teach me sign language because they thought that I might need it when I got older.

I also never spoke when I was around my teachers, although I did talk when I was alone with my parents. Every time my mother and father tried to tell the teachers that I did not need to learn sign language, they were skeptical.

Then one day at school, a cup of chocolate pudding was placed in front of me. I said to them what seemed to be "I don't want it!" The teachers then started to believe what my parents were saying. From then on, I just kept on fooling them by talking very little.

The teachers at Thomas Wildey tested my reflexes and balance by laying me on my stomach on top of a large rubber ball. They pushed the ball back and forth to see if I would put my arms out to catch myself without falling off the ball.

My parents were beginning to get a little worried about me because every time they tried to put me on the floor to crawl around, I did not even try to move, but just stayed right where I was. It was then they decided to contact the neurosurgeon. One of his first comments was that I might end up being mentally retarded.

However, things started to change. When I was about a year old, my mother carried me into the living room, placed me on the floor and walked out. About five minutes later when she came back into the room, she was surprised to discover that I was no longer in the same place.

I had crawled behind a chair in the living room. I guess that I was driven by curiosity and wanted to wander around the room, which is normal for young children, and in case you are wondering, I was not hurt when I moved behind the chair.

When my parents discovered that I had moved from one place to another on my own, they were very happy. They informed the doctors of this at Children's Hospital the next time that they took me to the MM clinic. (MM stands for Myelomeningocele). The MM Clinic is set up at the hospital to provide for various doctors to get together and meet with children that have disabilities, and their parents.

Getting these doctors together enables them to discuss the individuals' needs and to help parents deal with their children who have physical and/or mental disabilities. It also allows them to coordinate efforts in order to help them make more decisions that are confident and it gives them the chance to keep up on how things are going.

One of my most outstanding memories about being at Thomas Wildey School involved an accident in which I fell out of my wheelchair. My classmates and I were going outside -- to fly kites. One of the kids from my class was pushing my wheelchair, and apparently not paying attention, because my wheelchair flipped over the sidewalk.

The next thing I remember is looking up and seeing a bus right in front of me. I was taken back into the school clinic for a checkup and they called my mother to come and pick me up from school. After we arrived home, she discovered a few pebbles stuck in my forehead. Most of the pebbles were easy to take out because they were not that deep. Eventually my mother got all of the pebbles pulled out of my forehead and decided that I did not need to go to the hospital for medical treatment.

5

PHYSICAL THERAPY

When I was about three months old, my doctors suggested to my mother and father that they should begin physical therapy on my legs to loosen up the tendons in my ankles and knees so that they would not start to tighten up.

When I was about four years old, I had surgery to cut the tendons in my ankles and knees to release some of the tension that had built up. Having this surgery also made it easier for me to be able to wear leg braces, which would help strengthen my arms. I cannot use my legs at all because I am paralyzed from the waist down as I had mentioned earlier but I do have upper body strength.

During the day while I was at school, I had physical therapy until I was in the sixth grade. I did some arm exercises each day with a physical therapist to help keep my strength up.

At the time, I thought that all of that physical therapy was a waste of time. I guess it wasn't because it made me a lot stronger now than I use to be. The thing that I liked best about physical therapy was that I got to get out of class.

I also had occupational therapy, which was fun because it involved activities such as drawing and playing with wooden blocks.

For the first five years of school, I was put into a special OH (orthopedically handicapped) class. In 1988, when I was eight years old, I started first grade at Batavia Elementary School.

The first year at Batavia Elementary, I was still in the OH class, but when I was about nine or 10 years old and in the second grade, I was mainstreamed into regular classes. I was one of the first kids in my OH class to be mainstreamed.

Every year, the school that I was attending would have to update what is referred to as an Individual Education Plan (IEP) for mentally and physically handicapped children. This was done to follow my progress throughout my life in and out of school. This IEP is just like a progress report because the teachers would ask me how I was doing and how things were going so they would also know what I was capable of doing.

They would also have a physical therapist come in and talk to my parents and me about doing physical therapy at school, how much physical therapy and what kind was necessary to do at school and at home.

Besides physical therapy, I was also involved with Stepping-Stones for about one year. This is a swimming program for mentally and/or physically handicapped children. Occasionally I would go there with my mother for swimming lessons. She would always help me out when I was in the water. I still need help when I go swimming because I have not yet learned how to swim on my own.

Another problem that I had as a young child was being afraid of loud noises. Every time I heard a loud noise,

I would start to cry, and I did not stop crying until the noise was turned off. So every time someone used a vacuum cleaner or blender, or was making any other kind of noise, I had to be taken into another room so that I would not be able to hear it as loud. Even the music from the radio or piano bothered me. That problem went on until I was about three or four years old; now that I am older, there are hardly any noises that bother me.

I also used to have a gag reflex when I tried to eat food, which still bothers me sometimes. Until I was about five years old, I could not eat anything without gagging and getting sick, so my parents fed me things like baby formula, eggnog and small portions of food, then I started to eat food without getting sick. I still have some problems with getting sick when I eat or drink certain things.

During my first three years, I didn't grow much. Because I didn't grow out of my clothes very fast, my mother and father didn't have to keep buying me new clothes.

6

ON MY OWN

When I was in the fourth grade, I got a perfect score on every one of my spelling tests and was an honor roll student. As soon as I entered the fifth grade, I was no longer in an OH class. I was able to do things on my own, and I was placed into a normal classroom. I was physically capable of doing just about anything. Since then, that is the way things have been. I did well, too, in the sixth grade, but I had trouble with my grades in reading class. When I was in the eighth grade, I was once again an honor roll student and I and passed two of the four parts of the Proficiency Test.

By ninth grade, I passed the other two parts. I started my first year in high school in the fall of 1996, and to be honest, my grades were not as good as they were when I was in elementary school and the eighth grade. They weren't too bad because I had enough credits to pass and proceed to the tenth grade. Everyone has probably had a few bad grades every now and then and everyone makes mistakes.

Part of the reason I was not doing too well that year was because of the surgery to revise my shunt. As I said in Chapter three, this surgery was done during my freshman year.

Because of this surgery, I missed a lot of school during the year. I frequently left school early because I was getting headaches or became sick. I was also having a hard time concentrating on my schoolwork.

I was also having trouble in school because some of the subjects that I was taking were just plain hard. For example, I had completely failed algebra class during my freshman year, so I had to take it over again during my sophomore year, as did a lot of other people in my class.

My algebra teacher was concerned that I was not ready to re-take algebra during my sophomore year because she was afraid that I might fail again. Instead of algebra, they rearranged my schedule to place me into a different type of math class. The three classes that I had the hardest time with during my freshman year were algebra, English I, and German I.

During my freshman and sophomore years in high school, I only had four subjects per quarter, but in the third and fourth quarters, we switched and took four different classes, which actually meant I was taking eight classes a year. Each of my classes lasted about 85 minutes. The classes that I took during my freshman year were General Algebra I, German I, Business and Consumer, keyboarding and computer applications, physical science, physical education, art foundations, and English I.

As a sophomore, I took Parenting, which lasted for only one quarter, German II, Mixed Chorus, which was a fun class, Applied Biology, Health, which is the class that followed my Parenting class, Accounting, English II, and Drawing and Painting I.

During my junior and senior year, I went to a vocational school. I took Computerized Business

Technology, a class that is designed to show people how to operate certain software programs and an exciting class to be taking if you like computers.

After I graduated from high school, in June of 2000, I decided that I wanted to go to college and become a computer programmer.

In January 2001, I began attending the University of Cincinnati Clermont College majoring in Computer Information Systems Technology (CIS). In June 2003, I will have an Associates of Applied Business degree. My oldest nephew, Gary, graduated from Bethel Tate High School as well as Grant Joint Vocational School in 2001 and in the fall of 2001, he began attending the University of Cincinnati Clermont College. My niece, Jenny is also a student at the University of Cincinnati Clermont College.

During my freshman and sophomore year in high school, I had to get up around 5:30 a.m., and it usually took me about an hour to get ready for school, so I was on the school bus around 6:30 a.m. and at school by 7:00 a.m.

School began around 7:30 a.m and I usually arrived ten or fifteen minutes early, so I had to wait on the bus until around 7:20 a.m. when the other buses arrived. The bus that I rode is handicap accessible so when they got me on the bus, they could simply strap my wheelchair down so that it would not move around on the bus.

Every morning when I got to school, I would go right to my locker to put my coat away, and then I would go to my first class. Most of the time, the hallways would be crowded, which made it a little difficult for me to get through to my next class.

My teachers allowed me to leave before the next class started so that I could avoid the crowds in the hallways and get to my next class on time. This helped me out because I had to sit and wait for the elevator, which sometimes took a couple of minutes.

My teachers also gave me one book for keeping at school and one book for keeping at home so that I didn't have to carry a heavy schoolbag on the back of my wheelchair all day long. I tried to carry my books around school during my freshman year but to tell you the truth, I was happier when I had a locker even though I only used it for my coat. I could have used a locker when I was a freshman but at the time, I told them that I didn't want to use one. We were only given approximately five minutes to get to the next class. Anytime we had a fire drill at school or some other kind of emergency, I had no way of getting out of the building by myself. I would have to be picked up out of my wheelchair by an adult, which would usually be a teacher, and then I would be carried outside, which was kind of embarrassing but they only did it when it was really necessary. During my junior and senior year, I was able to get myself out of the building for emergencies because the vocational school that I attended has only one floor.

Every day after school, I would get on my bus about 15 minutes before everyone else so that my bus could get back in time to pick up the elementary kids. When I got home from school, someone would drive down the driveway to meet me at the school bus. My mother was usually the one who came to get me because my father was at work. He has since retired but I will tell you more about that in Chapter Seven.

When I came home from school, I got myself a snack and watched some television or played a game on the computer for about an hour or so before I did my homework. My snack was usually cookies and something to drink. Sometimes I watch television or listen to the radio and do my homework at the same time.

My friends and teachers at school do not seem to mind that I am handicapped because they seem to have an idea of what it is like to be handicapped and they can understand how hard it is sometimes to do certain things. My teachers and friends are always there when I need their help. I have had some of the best teachers any student could ask for and I am very grateful to them.

7

MY FAMILY AND ME

I have a large family with five sisters, and three brothers. Currently, I have seven nephews, and nineteen nieces. They all mean a lot to me.

My brother Donnie and his wife Liz have one son named Robert, and three daughters whose names are Hollyann, Cecilia, and Rebeca.

My brother Raymond and his wife Leandra have five daughters. Their names are Nicole, Lura, Anita, Cheryll, and Wendy. Raymond is also my Godfather.

My brother Andy, who was in the Marine Corps., and his wife Crystal have two daughters whose names are Kelsey and Savannah, who was born in October 2002. They also have a son named Andrew.

My sister Rosanne and her husband Gary have one son named Gary and five daughters whose names are Leah, Jenny, Aimee, Debbie, and Kelsey. Leah is only about a month younger than I am.

My sister Marie and her husband Nick have two daughters named Isabella and Miriam and a son named Lucas, who was born in July 2000.

My sister Louise and her husband James have one son named Jonathan and a daughter named Olivia, who was born on July 12, 2000. I am the Godfather of both Olivia and Lucas.

My sister Judy is a single mother with one daughter whose name is Charlene, and two sons named Zachary and Michael.

My sister Elizabeth and her husband Ryan have one daughter named Liberty who was born on June 5, 2002. Ryan is in the Air Force and he and Elizabeth are currently living in Germany on a temporary basis. Elizabeth and I both went to school at New Richmond High School as freshman and sophomores and graduated in the year 2000. Instead of staying at New Richmond High School, I decided to finish the rest of my high school years at Grant Career Center, which is the vocational school that I mentioned earlier.

My father's name is Donald. He was a Sr. Mechanical Application's Engineer and had been working in the field of machine tools since he was 17 years old. He took early retirement but after two weeks, he went back to continue working temporarily as a consultant.

My mother's name is Joyce. Before she and my father got married in 1961, she was in nursing school for about three months studying to become a surgical nurse. Since she has been married to my father, she has been a homemaker, mother, and a grandmother.

As you can see, I have a rather large family, and as I said before, they all are very special and they mean a lot to me.

We have many family gatherings at my house such as celebrating birthday parties and Christmas, which is my favorite time of the entire year. We always celebrate Christmas together at my house.

The family gatherings are always a riot and a lot of fun. Every once in a while, when the weather is warm, we go outside, sit by a campfire, and roast hot dogs and marshmallows. My family has always been very helpful and supportive, and I like it when they come and visit.

Sometimes for fun, I like to tease my nieces and nephews, but they don't seem to mind. My wheelchair seems to fascinate some of my younger nieces and nephews because they like to play around with it.

If I had to decide, I think that the best advice I ever received was from my mother and father, and that was to "Keep up the good work." In my opinion, when people think of or hear the word "handicapped" or "disability," or even see someone who is handicapped, they automatically start to think of that person as being incapable of doing anything on their own. Then again, you could say that there are many people who don't think that way. My friends and family have always tried to be supportive. They treat me as if I am not handicapped and have never once made fun of my condition. That is one thing keeps me going.

Almost every time that I go out to the store or some other place, children sometimes do stare at me. Many times when a young girl or boy stares at me, I notice their mom or dad whispering to them. I think they tell them that they should not stare, which is a good thing but I think they stare because they are young and curious and don't understand why I am in a wheelchair. I have been in a few situations where they just come right up to me and wave or say "Hi". When they do, I just say hi back.

I always try to think to myself, that if someone doesn't like you for who you are or what you are, then they are not the kind of people that you would want to be around or should even have as friends.

When I was in the sixth grade, my class, and in fact, the entire sixth grade went on a fieldtrip to a place called "Camp Joy," and I wanted to go with them. My teacher called to tell my mother that she thought that I wouldn't be able to go on the fieldtrip because I wouldn't be able to participate in some activities and therefore wouldn't have any fun. That made my parents and me angry. However, the school principal called back shortly after my teacher talked to him. Somehow, he found out about what my teacher had said to my mother on the phone and he said that no matter what he had to do, he would make sure that I would be able to go on this fieldtrip with my classmates and have a good time, which I did!

When I was younger, my bedroom was on the second floor. Now it is on the first floor of our two-story house. It was difficult for my parents to carry me up and down the steps, so they moved my bedroom to a converted ground-floor room. Having my bedroom on the first floor makes things a lot easier on me, too. A small section of my bedroom was converted into a bathroom built by my father and I that is handicap accessible.

I have always lived on a farm, which used to be a dairy farm many years ago. I have five horses: a filly named My Tie, a colt named Milwaukee, Bonnie, and Babe, who is the mother of the My Tie and Milwaukee, and Jadavodka, who we call J.V. for short. I have two cats, Frankie and Miss Kitty. I have one bird whose name is Paradise; three dogs whose names are Red, Cindy and Penny; and a rabbit named Daisy.

The only animals that I take care of are the bird and the rabbit, and my parents help me a lot since it is hard for me to get out to her cage, especially during the winter. I really like animals. When I was younger, we had a lot of chickens, goats and cows but all of those animals either passed away or we gave or sold them to someone else.

One of the things that I like to do is watch television. I have my own television in my room and my favorite sports to watch on television are gymnastics, baseball, football, and sometimes basketball. I like to talk on the phone with my friends and spend time with them, especially while I am at school. I also like to play games on my computer and on my Nintendo 64, which I do just about everyday.

I have a collection of more than 500 baseball cards. My favorite baseball team is the Cincinnati Reds. I have been to many Cincinnati Reds baseball games and I have a collection of baseballs and pictures. I also collect Cincinnati Reds baseball caps and I watch them on television all the time.

My favorite football team is the Cincinnati Bengals. One of these days, I hope to go and see a Cincinnati Bengals football game. I have a large collection of model cars, most of which are antiques. I also enjoy assembling model cars myself, but I don't have quite as many of those.

I never played in a school sport, but I did play on a softball team in 1991 and 1993, and I have two softball trophies. When I look at my softball trophies, I wish that I were still playing. I don't play softball anymore but I still practice at home whenever I get a chance. I remember once in a softball game--when a hard-hitting batter came up to bat, someone had to stand in front of me for protection. The coaches were afraid that the ball might hit me because I would not be able to move out of the way fast enough to avoid being hit.

Even though one of the coaches stood in front of me, I was hit by the ball in my right arm as I stuck it out to catch the ball. They were going to take me out of the game but I told them that I would be all right and that my arm wasn't really hurting much. I have never played basketball on a team but I do occasionally practice and shoot hoops when I have a chance. One day I hope to play on a basketball team and I hope to get back to playing softball, too, but I guess I will have to see what happens.

I like to listen to the radio, CD's and tapes. My favorite kind of music is country music. I listen to the radio as I am doing my homework and I keep the radio on when I sleep at night.

Some of my favorite country music singers are Garth Brooks, Reba McEntire, George Strait, LeAnn Rimes, and Lila McCann. In April 1999, Lila came to New Richmond High School and did a concert for the entire school. It was so much fun. The one country song that I really like, which makes me emotional most of the time when I hear it, is a song by the group Alabama called "Angels Among Us."

I guess it makes me emotional because it is a song that I can relate to. Sometimes when I hear that song, I start to cry for a few minutes and I ask myself the one question that people like me might ask themselves when they have to deal with the same problems that I do: "Why me?" Almost everyday, I would stop and think about what it would be like to walk and not be in a wheelchair. I sometimes get angry or frustrated because of the things that I have to do or can't do because of my disability. Being in a wheelchair can be fun especially if you know how to go really fast.

Sometimes, I don't even think about my disability. Instead of thinking about the things that I can't do, I think about the things that I can do. If there is something that I really want to do, I usually will try to figure out a way of doing it because I am a fighter, not a quitter.

I also like to go fishing even if I don't catch anything, which happens to me a lot. I usually go fishing once a year with my father or somebody else. Going on vacation is fun, too. As I mentioned earlier, my brother Andy was in the Marines, so my parents, my sister Elizabeth and I went to Parris Island, South Carolina, to see him when he graduated from boot camp. We also went to Camp LeJuene, North Carolina, where he was stationed in 1997. While we were there, we took a side trip to Myrtle Beach, South Carolina.

Just about every summer or sometime during the year I go on vacation with my parents. So far, I have been to Gatlinburg Tennessee; North Carolina; South Carolina and all of the states that border Ohio. Someday, I would like to go to Disneyland.

One time I got tickets to go see the Olympic gymnasts who won the gold medal at the Summer Games in 1996. They were called the Magnificent Seven. My parents, my niece Aimee and I had to drive to Dayton, Ohio, to the competition, but we did not have to pay for the tickets because I had called the Sunshine Foundation and told them that I wanted to meet the gold medal gymnastics team, so gave us the tickets along with hotel room reservations and spending money.

We went to see the competition but when we got there something got mixed up so we didn't get to sit in the front row at floor level, which is where we expected to sit. Instead, we were sitting up high, which made it hard to see, but it was still fun. After the competition, we went backstage to go meet the gymnasts. We got their autographs, took pictures, and then went back to our hotel.

The next morning, we went back home. This was the second time I had seen the gymnasts perform in person. The first time was in Cincinnati, Ohio but we did not have backstage passes to meet them that time.

8

THE SPECIAL OLYMPICS

"Let me win. But if I cannot win, let me be brave in the attempt." That is the Special Olympic motto.

In 1988, I was eight years old when I became involved with competing in the Special Olympics. Actually, I was invited through the school to attend the Special Olympics before 1988, but my parents had decided to wait for a while to sign me up because they were not sure if they wanted me to be in it or not.

The Special Olympics were always held in Milford, Ohio, in the month of April, but since 1996, they have been held in New Richmond, Ohio. One year that I competed, it rained a lot but I am not exactly sure what year it was. I only competed for about eight years but got back into it, as you will see later on in the chapter. Each time I competed in two events.

I don't have any official records on my competitions in the Special Olympics, but what I do have are the medals that I won. The events that I competed in were events like the softball throw and wheelchair races, from which I have gold, silver and bronze medals.

I would still be in the Special Olympics but we were told that I could not be because I was not mentally retarded, which makes no sense because I was not mentally retarded to begin with. I spoke with the person in charge of the Special Olympics, and was told that there is no reason that I could not compete in the Special Olympics. I had not competed in the Special Olympics since 1996, but in May 1999, I got back into the Special Olympics and competed in the 25-meter dash and the softball throw winning a gold medal in both events and having my picture placed in the school newspaper. In 2000 and 2001, I competed in the same events, but in 2002, I did not compete because the Special Olympics were not held in New Richmond.

9

A Weekend in Columbus

From Friday, August 6, 1999 to Sunday, August 8, 1999, I attended the first annual Leadership Forum for students with disabilities in Columbus, Ohio. I learned about this forum from a staff member at Grant Career Center when I was a junior. I was given papers to fill out and send in, and I was also expected to write an essay explaining why I should be chosen as a delegate for the forum, why I was interested in going, to explain a little bit about myself and the things that I like to do, and discuss what my future plans were. After writing the essay, I eagerly awaited a response. Within weeks, I received a letter saying that they wanted to interview me for the forum. The interview was done right at school, and afterward, I was told that I would be contacted by mail as to whether or not I had accepted. As it turns out, I received a letter of congratulations. Words cannot explain how happy I was to be selected as a delegate. I was driven to Columbus by my parents and dropped off at the forum. There were a total of 23 delegates, and it was interesting to see that none of them had the same disability that I did. Many of them had situations worse than mine, and I thought, "I'm glad I'm not them".

Once everyone had signed in, we were divided into small groups. In these small groups, we did a lot of paper work. We also had large group sessions where all the small groups would get together each day to hear different speakers talk about their disabilities and how they handle them. It was exciting to hear the things they had to say.

Saturday night, a dance was held for all of the delegates. Sunday, we went to the Capitol building for a tour, and then we went to the Hyatt Regency Hotel where our final speaker was Ted Kennedy, Jr. Ted came over and shook my hand, and then sat down next to me, and ate his lunch. That was one of the most wonderful experiences in my life. I am very grateful to have had the chance to meet him. I was sad to see the forum come to an end because I met a lot of nice people. However, I know that I will be able to keep in touch with them because our Program Specialist sent a paper that has all of the names, addresses, phone numbers, and email addresses of all the delegates.

All meals were provided free of charge as well as the dorms where we slept. The next year, I applied to be a counselor at the second annual Youth Leadership Forum but was not selected. I was also given the opportunity to participate in the National Leadership Forum, which is held every year in Washington, DC. Unfortunately, I was not selected but I did hear that many others who were invited were chosen. I hope that next year when I apply, I will be selected.

10

GOING TO THE HOSPITAL

Since I was born, I have gone to the hospital for various reasons. About once every six months, I would go to the hospital for clinic so that my doctors could get an idea of what and how I was doing. Now that I am older, I only need to go to clinic once a year.

The clinic date is always set up by the hospital but if we cannot attend on the assigned date then we just call them up and have it changed. I have four doctors I normally see when I go to clinic: a neurologist, an orthopedic specialist, a urologist and one other person who is not a doctor but comes in just to see how things are going with me and to see if I need anything.

I have had 15 surgeries and my legs were broken many times. I think that Children's Hospital is the best hospital, which is why I go there to have surgery and other things done if necessary. Children's Hospital is also one of the only hospitals that will do surgery and provide special treatment for children and young adults with disabilities.

The doctors at Children's Hospital keep close records of things that my parents and I tell them, which is what they do when I go to the hospital for clinic in addition to my medical history. The people who work at Children's

Hospital have always said that they are very shocked and astonished at how far I have come in such a short time taking into account all of the things I have had to go through in the past because of my disability.

In April 1994, I had surgery for a lazy eye. Glasses were prescribed to help correct it earlier, but the surgery still had to be done. After the surgery, I wore a patch on my eye until it healed.

In March 1996, I was admitted to the hospital for about a week because of a strange problem with my leg. The doctors couldn't tell what it was right away, but eventually, it was diagnosed as cellulites in my right lower leg, which was treated with antibiotics.

Over the years, I have spent a lot of time in the hospital, and every time, I wanted to get home as soon as possible so that I could finish the other things that I really enjoyed doing or needed to be done.

11

GETTING MY DRIVER'S LICENSE

A few people have been asking me how I will be able to drive a car. In August 2001, I got my temporary driver's license, and I will be getting my permanent license as soon as I take the driving test, which will be different than normal because of all the adjustments that have to be made. When I do get a driver's license, a vehicle will have to be specially designed for me with hand controls.

I was not able to get my driver's license at the time because I had surgery to help straighten up my back so that I would have better balance when driving a car.

This surgery was done differently than my other two back surgeries. The rods that the doctors put in my back this time were placed differently in order to provide more and better support. They bent the rods in order to make them stronger.

When I got a new wheelchair in May 1997, my seat cushion was designed with a gel inside it and removable hip guards. The hip guards are placed on the top and they had Velcro on them, which helped to hold them in place.

The hip guards that I had inside my seat cushion were placed on the right side to help me keep my balance. It didn't work as well as I expected, but it did help me a little. A few years later, I got a new wheelchair with supports on both sides of the chair to help me sit up straighter.

To get my permanent driver's license, I will need to get my wheelchair modified so that I can use it in the handicapped-accessible van that I will be driving. I was tested out in a car but when I got in the driver's seat, I couldn't see enough of the road so we decided that a van would be better for me. It was also determined that a plastic brace should be made to help me with keeping my balance because I no longer have the support from the rods and the bone fusion that was done in March 1998. I had my first actual driving lesson in the early part of 2002. I drove around the hospital parking lot for a couple of hours and had a lot of fun. I am excited about having my own van. I will be sitting in my wheelchair when I drive because a regular driver's seat does not provide enough support because of my scoliosis.

The spinal surgery that I had was not absolutely necessary, but I think that having this surgery was just the best thing to do. I chose to have this surgery for obvious reasons.

My doctors told me was that if I did decide to have this surgery, it could cause me to get pneumonia, which is an inflammation of the lungs.

I chose to have this surgery to enable me to have better control of my wheelchair and my car when I finally get my driver's license.

In addition, if I did have this surgery, then it would make doing the things that I want to do, easier, such as driving a car, which by the way, makes me very excited. Having the surgery made me able to breathe better and sit up straighter than I could before and ride the horses on the farm better than before. I decided to have this surgery at that time because I didn't want to have to worry about it later on. My doctors could have done this surgery on me when I was much younger. They decided not to do the surgery because that they thought that the surgery wasn't really necessary to do at the time.

After I had the surgery, I had to stay at home and do my schoolwork working with a home tutor because the doctor said that I would have to be in a body cast for at least six months but he changed his mind about that and instead, I wore a plastic brace for a few months. The surgery was done on March 6, 1998. On the last day of my sophomore year, I went to school to see my friends. There was also an awards assembly that I attended. I did not receive any awards during my freshman, year so I was hoping that I would get something for my sophomore year. Fortunately, I did receive an award. It was a medal for outstanding achievement, and my former physical education teacher presented it. When I went up to receive my medal, everyone in the gymnasium, where the assembly was held was cheering and clapping for me, which is not something I had expected. It was the only award that I received that year, but that was good enough for me.

Before I had this surgery, which I am glad to have over with, I had to see many doctors in order to make sure that nothing would go wrong during the surgery. First, I went to see my family doctor so they could determine I was healthy enough to have this surgery.

If there were any reason that I would get sick before the surgery, it would have had to be postponed until I was better because the doctors will not do surgery unless you are in perfect health. I also had to take some iron pills up until the day that I had the surgery in order to make my blood stronger.

I'm glad that I didn't get sick before I had the surgery because I had been waiting a long time to have this surgery. The day before the surgery, I had to go and see the surgeon to have some tests.

Deciding whether to have this surgery now or to wait until later was difficult. Actually, it took me about two or three weeks to think about it until I finally made my decision.

Before I had the surgery, I could hardly believe and did not want to believe what my doctor said about the sacrifices that I would have to make if I wanted to have this surgery.

When I asked my parents to call the doctor to schedule an appointment for me to go and talk to him about the surgery. The main reason I decided to have the surgery was that I was angry because I would keep losing my balance and falling over.

After talking to my doctor and telling him that I wanted to have the surgery, I started to have second thoughts because my doctor was telling me that I would be out of school for the rest of the school year, and it would cause me to put off getting my driver's license.

After I thought about it more, I began to realize that these sacrifices would be worth making, because after I recover from the surgery, I would be able to do the things better that I have wanted to do, such as getting my driver's license. I would also no longer have to worry about losing my balance. Unfortunately, the rods had to be removed due to an infection, which I will tell you about later on, which caused me to lose my balance.

Before they did the surgery, my doctors did tell me

that they would not be able to tell how well things would be until after the surgery.

As you are reading this, you might be asking, "Was he scared about having this surgery?" My answer to that question is both yes no. I wasn't afraid about having this surgery because I am used to having surgery, so I knew what to expect.

The thing that scared me was that I had to have many blood tests both before and after I had the surgery and I always get a little worked up when they have to stick a needle into my arm. Of course, I was also hoping that nothing would go wrong.

12

MY THIRD SPINAL SURGERY

About a week before I was scheduled to have the surgery on my back, my mother and father drove me to the hospital to talk to my doctor about the surgery. The things that my doctor talked about were things that he would be doing when he performs the surgery, and after I talked to him, I felt much better.

We arrived at the hospital early, so we waited in the car until it was time to go inside, and then we sat in the waiting room and waited. My doctor was running a little behind schedule because we were sitting in the waiting room for an hour longer than we expected.

However, we finally went in to talk to my doctor. When we did, the first thing that he did was ask himself what he was going to do, because he said that doing this surgery would not be easy. He told us that what he will do is place two steel rods in my back that would be bent in an L shape.

The rods are bent like that so that he can insert them into the sacrum, which are the two holes at the bottom of the pelvis bone, which would help prevent the rods from breaking. My doctor's biggest concern was getting the rods to go through the sacrum without causing an injury to a blood vessel or anything else.

After my doctor told us that he would be putting rods in my back, which are about a half-inch in diameter and are stainless steel, he told us that he would also do a bone fusion to help strengthen the rods. He said that he would not remove the rods in my back from the previous surgeries because it was not necessary. He also said that I should have more x-rays to give him a better idea of what my spinal curvature looks like.

Just before we went over to have the x-rays, I remember that I started to get upset about the things that might happen to me, but after a while, I calmed down so that I could have the x-rays taken. The next day, I went to the hospital to have some breathing tests and blood tests, and to have my heart checked to see if everything was all right. I also had to have a physical examination before the surgery, which is a typical thing for all surgeries.

On March 6, 1998, I got up around 4:00 a.m. because I had to be at the hospital at 6:00 a.m. and it takes an hour to get to the hospital. We got to the hospital on time and spent about 30 minutes waiting, another 45 minutes talking to the doctor and the nurse and answering and asking questions. At 7:15 a.m., the doctors started getting me ready for the surgery.

A friend of mine from school gave me a small prayer cloth long before the surgery. I took that with me to the hospital and I kept it with me the whole time.

The surgery lasted approximately 14 hours during which the doctors say they didn't leave the room for any reason, but, at different times throughout the procedure, my doctors contacted my mother and father about what they were doing and how I was doing.

The first report was about the work that they did on my abdomen, which was about two hours after the doctors had put me to sleep. Approximately two and a half hours later, they were finished with that and contacted my mother and father again to tell them that they were going to start working on my back putting in the rods. Before the rods were put in, the discs in my back were removed and the bones were cut in order for my spine to be stretched out. Approximately two and a half hours later, they came out again to tell my mother and father that I was still doing all right and that they were going to release the tendons in the right side of my leg down by my pelvis. Again, they told my mother and father that I was doing all right. Then they started on working on my upper lumbar area and about two hours later, they started to put the rods in my back. They were considering taking out the old rods but instead they just put the new rods right below the old ones and clamped them together.

Putting the rods in took about three hours because the doctors could not get them to stay where they were supposed to stay, so they ended up taking those rods out and putting new ones in. After the surgery was over my doctor showed x-rays to my mother and father and told them that they could not get the entire curve out of my back because it has been there too long and a lot of the bone structure was too weak.

Around 9:30 p.m., I began waking up from the surgery. I remember that when I woke up, I was so cold that I was shivering. I was also very sleepy, and I was calling for my mother and father. Around 10:00 p.m., my mother and father came in to the Intensive Care Unit (ICU) to see me. My mother spent the night in the hospital with me, but not in the same room. By Sunday, I was taken out of ICU and put into a regular room, where I stayed for the next three days. Every day my mother and father came up to see me. Many of my other relatives also came to see me while I was in the hospital.

I became sick to my stomach, so my doctors had to insert a tube down my nose to help get rid of the fluid in my stomach, but by the next day, it was taken out. My doctors originally planned to do another surgery to release the tendons, but had decided it wasn't necessary. My doctors thought that I could be in the hospital from ten days to two weeks, but only six days after my operation I was released from the hospital and sent home.

Exactly five weeks, after my third spinal surgery, I had to be taken back to the hospital for additional surgery because the fluid draining from my back had become infected. The only way to get rid of the infection was to surgically drain out the infected fluid.

That surgery took less than one hour, but I spent the weekend in the hospital, which happened to be the weekend of Easter Sunday. During that time, I was given antibiotics through an IV and then was sent home.

Instead of leaving the IV in, it was replaced with something called a PICC line. The PICC line is a very small rubber tube that is placed into the arm into a vein and goes all the way up to the heart. (The PICC line can be placed into either arm or another place in the body depending on the situation, but I had mine in my right arm). This PICC line is also safer than an IV because it rarely gets infected. I was given antibiotics through the PICC line for approximately eight weeks.

My doctors were planning to put me in a body cast for six months and then a plastic brace for another six months. Instead of doing that, they just made a brace for me and decided not to put me in a body cast. That made me very happy because that made doing things a lot easier.

I had to have assistance when I changed my clothes because I was not allowed to sit up. When I was out of my brace, I could not sit up at all. My brace was made not to sit me up all the way, but I was allowed to sit about half way and roll from side to side. I also used a specially designed wheelchair that had an adjustable back on it so it could be raised or lowered when it was necessary. When I could not sit up completely, my mother and father rearranged my bedroom at home so that I could get to things a little easier.

Approximately three weeks after the second surgery, I went to the doctor again to get a few x-rays. He decided that it was time for me to sit up a little bit higher than before. I went to the doctor again to have the stitches in my back taken out. That time he told me I could sit up all the way.

About a year following my third spinal surgery, urologists performed a cystoscopy, which is a diagnostic test to visualize the lower urinary tract (bladder and urethra). A device called a cystoscope is inserted into the bladder through the urethra, which allows the surgeon to look inside. Water then flows through the cystoscope, which expands the bladder and urethra as well as the urethral openings into the bladder.

Cystoscopies take anywhere from ten to thirty minutes and are almost always done on an outpatient basis involving a general anesthetic. Before the procedure, I spoke with my anesthesiologist and asked him if it was necessary to use general anesthetic since I have no feeling from the waist down. The reason for using general anesthesia is to prevent hypertension, which causes blood pressure to rise and could cause the patient to become alarmed. The cystoscopy was done to detect a false passage in my bladder.

In August 1999, I developed more problems with infection in my back. It all started when I was on vacation in Gatlinburg, Tennessee. When I returned home from Gatlinburg, my mother called the hospital and they told her to take me to the emergency room where they put me on IV antibiotics just like the last time I had an infection in my back. Surgery was done to remove the rods at the bottom of my back that were put in when I had my first spinal surgery. The surgery lasted about two hours, and I was sent home two days later. After I returned home, a pressure sore was found from sitting and I was unable to go to school until it healed.

Approximately three weeks after I went back to school, I was put into the hospital again because of a staph infection. Staphylococcus is a type of organism on the surface of the skin, and if a person should happen to have an open cut or, in my case, an open sore, the organism can get inside and become an infection. When I was diagnosed with a staph infection, doctors found signs of it in my blood, in my urine and in my back.

My neurosurgeon came by to examine the shunt I had in my head and told my parents and me that it had to be removed because it might be the source of the staph infection. That surgery had to be put off for two weeks because while I was in the hospital being treated for the staph infection, I was taking Ibuprofen for headaches, which might cause me to hemorrhage, so they sent me home for about two weeks to allow the medication to clear out of my system. Before sending me home, they put in another PICC line and I had to have IV antibiotics to keep the infection down. This time, the PICC line was placed into my left arm. Toward the end of October 1999, I was brought back in to have the shunt taken out. The shunt was then cultured to see if any type of infection would grow, which it didn't. After about three days, I was sent back home.

The next month, I got sick again and had to go back to the hospital. That time it was for a viral infection and I spent about a week in the hospital while being treated for that.

A few weeks later, I had another surgery to remove more rods that were put in my back from a previous surgery because doctors thought that those rods could also be a source of the staph infection. A bone biopsy was done at the same time and the culture of the bone biopsy was also negative. However, I was kept on the IV antibiotics until my back healed from the surgery.

In October 2000, I had my 15th surgery, which I hope will be my last, because here I am almost 22 years old and already I have had more surgeries than most people have had have in a lifetime. Having this surgery though, was probably one of the best decisions I have ever made. I say that because now I am more independent than I was before I had the procedure. It's called a mitroffinoff and a colostomy. The mitroffinoff was done to give me better control over going to the bathroom because I no longer have to lie down and instead I can just go to a toilet and do what I have to do. With the colostomy, I can just go and do what I need to do and not have to worry about accidents. However, the colostomy doesn't guarantee that I will not have to worry about an accident happening, it just lessens the chances of such an occurrence. The difference between the mitroffinoff and colostomy is quite simple. The mitroffinoff is for a catheter, which allows me to urinate, and the colostomy allows me to have bowel movements without any problems during the day. This procedure kept me in the hospital for 14 days, 10 of them in Intensive Care. Talking about this is embarrassing I admit, but after all, if I didn't have this done, I would not be as happy as I am now.

13

MY PERSONAL FEELINGS

Because of my disability, and everything that I have been through in the past I sometimes feel anger, frustration, sadness, and confusion.

Most of the time I feel really happy and good about myself. Actually, most of the time when I'm around a lot of people, I start to feel really happy and good about myself because I think that being around a lot of people can make a person feel good about themselves and make them forget about their own problems.

I have always felt that there is nothing worse than feeling bad about yourself, which is one thing that you do not ever want to have happen. Just like everyone else, I also like to go out, and I go out every chance that I can get.

Instead of using the word angry, I prefer to use the word frustrated because I think that the words angry and frustrated have very different definitions. If you were to look these words up in the dictionary, the definitions are probably just about the same, but not to me.

To me, the word angry is a word that would normally be used when I have something that has to be done, but do not want to do it. The one thing that I really hate doing is getting up early in the morning.

When I was younger, I would just go in my bedrooms and sometimes just sit in my bedroom and start crying for no reason, which I guess is where the words sad and frustrated come in. One of the main reasons that I would start to get emotional, was because I would always be thinking about the things that I would be able to do if I was never in a wheelchair.

I would also sometimes ask myself the question, "Why me?" and start crying. I occasionally still do ask myself that question and start to cry, but not as much as before.

One thing you could say about me is that I have a lot of friends in school because it seems like that there are a lot of people who know who I am, and they also seem to know my name. To me, having that kind of recognition, especially at school, is a real privilege, which I enjoy.

I would sometimes worry about being treated like everyone else. My friends have always treated me nicely, and they always help me out when I need it. There have been a couple of people who have been mean to me but I just try to forget about them.

I hope that you have had as much fun reading this book as I have had writing it, because in writing this autobiography, I have found out more about my disability than I knew before I started.

I hope that reading this autobiography has been a good learning experience for you, as it has been for me, which is the reason that I wanted to write this. I also hope that after you have finished reading this book, you have learned a thing or two, and that you will want to read it again.

If you want my advice, it doesn't matter who you are or what you are. Just NEVER, give up whatever it is you like to do. Whatever you do, you should not let a simple thing like a disability get in your way. I know that I will always keep on trying no matter what it takes and no matter what people say.

Being in a wheelchair like I am can sometimes be a lot of fun, but it can also make you feel sad at times because your ability to do things is limited, especially if you are paralyzed from the waist down like I am. I also hope that you will never have to face the same problems that I have had to deal with. Being in a wheelchair doesn't make me or anyone else in a wheelchair any different than anyone else.

Before I end this book, there are two things that I would like for you to remember. Always be positive, and stay that way. You may have found reading this book a little emotional, but I hope that you at least found it somewhat interesting.

Finally, I would like to thank my parents for everything that you have given to me and done for me. Without you and my brothers and sisters and nieces and nephews, I probably would not want to be here.

Things That Might Be Interesting To You

About Me

Animals: Our horses: Babe, JV, Bonnie, My Tie and Milwaukee.

Our dogs: Red, Cindy, Daisy and Penny.

My pet bird: Paradise

My pet rabbit: Daisy.

My favorite type of music: country music.

Some of my favorite country music singers: Garth Brooks, George Strait, LeAnn Rimes, Reba McEntire, and Lila McCann.

Favorite activities: playing softball, watching television, playing games on the computer, collecting baseball cards building model cars, and putting puzzles together.

Favorite sports: baseball, football, basketball, and gymnastics.

The place that I would like to go someday for a vacation: Disneyland.

My plans for after I graduate from high school: going to college and becoming a computer programmer.

Some of my favorite foods: pizza, hamburgers, French fries (with ketchup), mashed potatoes, and chicken.

My favorite snacks: anything with chocolate, cookies, cake, ice cream, potato chips, cookies, pumpkin and apple pie.

My favorite color: red.

Works Cited

(Some information from outside sources in this book were used.)

"Yes You Can" A Kit for Teens
The Spina Bifida Association pg. 4, 9, 28, 29.

Current Application of Laser-Assisted Neuroendoscopy Using the KTP/532 Wavelength.

Larry, J.M., Edmonds, L.D. Prevalence of Spina Bifida at birth-U.S., 1983-1990: a comparison of two surveillance systems. Morbidity and Morality.

Weekly Report, volume 45, number SS-2, April 19, 1996.

Recommendations for the use of folic acid to reduce the number of cases of Spina Bifida and other neural tube defects. Morbidity and Mortality Weekly Report, volume 41, number RR-14, September 11, 1992.

Menkes, J.H., Till, K., Gabriel, R.S., Malformations of the central nervous system, in Menkes, J.H., (ed.): Textbook of Child Neurology 4th edition, Philadelphia, Lea & Febiger, 1990, pg. 209-231.

Committee on Genetics. Folic acid for the prevention of neural tube defects. Pediatrics, volume 92, number 3, September 1993, pg. 493-494.

Luthy, D.A., et al. Cesarean section before the onset of labor and subsequent motor function in infants with Myelomeningocele diagnosed antenatally. The New England Journal of Medicine, volume 324, number 10, March 7, 1991, pg. 662-666.

Rotenstein, D., Reigel, D.H. Growth hormone treatment of children...the Journal of Pediatrics, volume 128, number 2.

Van der Put, N.M.J., et al. Mutated methylenetetrahydrofolate reductase as a risk factor for Spina Bifida. The Lancet, volume 346, October 21, 1995, pg. 1070-1071.

Children's Hospital Medical Center Division of Pediatric Urology Curtis Sheldon, M.D. Jeffrey Wacksman, M.D.

ISBN 1553950069-0

9 781553 950691

13062866R00038

Made in the USA
Lexington, KY
27 January 2012